RAF Helicopter
1970s and '80s

CHRIS GOSS

HISTORIC MILITARY AIRCRAFT SERIES, VOLUME 18

Published by Key Books
An imprint of Key Publishing Ltd
PO Box 100
Stamford
Lincs PE9 1XQ

www.keypublishing.com

The right of Chris Goss to be identified as the
author of this book has been asserted in accordance
with the Copyright, Designs and Patents Act 1988
Sections 77 and 78.

Copyright © Chris Goss, 2022

ISBN 978 1 80282 239 7

All rights reserved. Reproduction in whole or in part
in any form whatsoever or by any means is strictly
prohibited without the prior permission of the
Publisher.

Typeset by SJmagic DESIGN SERVICES, India.

Contents

Foreword

Flicking through this collection of helicopter photographs has brought back copious memories of operating numerous helicopter types across the globe. The most significant recollections are of those of the air, ground and support crews who enabled the job to be done. With the exception of helicopters working in either the Search and Rescue or Medivac roles, their mission is one of support to ground or maritime-based forces. The principle of 'what does the man on the ground need to achieve his mission and what is my part in that' remains apt for all aspects of rotary wing mission planning today.

All the platforms captured within the following photographs have been exploited by RAF Rotary Wing operators to deliver tactical and strategic capability in a plethora of operational theatres. While I have not flown the Whirlwind (it was withdrawn from RAF service prior to my first flight in a Gazelle at RAF Shawbury on 15 November 1983), it provided deployed tactical mobility to UK troops in theatres such as Malaya while delivering the vital life-saving UK Search and Rescue role.

I have flown many hours in the Wessex, Chinook and Puma, with a few on the Sea King. Each aircraft has its own nuance and has advantages over others in particular theatres of operation. For example, the Wessex's robust 'tail dragging' construct was ideal for the rough terrain and modus operandi of the Royal Ulster Constabulary and for supporting soldiers engaged in internal security duties on Operation *Banner* in Northern Ireland. Meanwhile, the Puma's rapid air transportability, limited downdraft and twin sliding door open cabin were just the job for the humanitarian aid delivery of Operation *Barwood* in Mozambique. The Sea King was an exceptionally suited platform for the frequent provision of rescue to Japanese squid fishermen and other maritime operators in the South Atlantic while based at Mount Pleasant Airfield in the Falkland Islands. I have enjoyed many hours flying on, and commanding operations on, these helicopters. However, without any doubt, the most capable, versatile and adaptable of all the helicopters that I have had the privilege to captain is the Chinook.

It is not Boeing that sells the Chinook to air forces around the world – it is what RAF operators do with it, demonstrating the limits of its capability, from -50°C to 50°C and from ground level to 14,000ft, in every corner of the globe. With 2,000 hours flown on the Chinook, the majority of which were with the Special Forces Flight of No. 7 Squadron, I have seen the mighty Chinook ensure the safe deployment and recovery of highly specialist troops engaged on strategically significant missions. There is nothing to rival the confidence boosting sound of a 'Wokka' as it is on short finals to recover troops, or its nimbleness as it perches commandingly over a GOPLAT (Gas and Oil Platform) while disgorging its payload.

Clearly, I am somewhat biased in my memories of the Chinook. However, I believe that it is the collective suite of helicopter platforms operated by the MOD that gives commanders effective choice in the selection of the most appropriate aircraft for the mission, something that held true in the 1970s and '80s and still does now more than ever before in 2022.

Air Marshal Sir Baz North, KBC OBE

Introduction

This book is the fifth in Key Publishing's series devoted to photographs of British combat aircraft of the 1970s and 1980s, the last two decades of the Cold War.

The first book in the series covered the Lightning and Phantom air defence aircraft, the second the Buccaneer and Vulcan bombers, while the third covered the Jaguar and Harrier ground-attack aircraft and the Sea Harrier. These were followed by a book on the reconnaissance and airborne early warning aircraft – the Shackleton, Nimrod, Canberra and Gannet. This book is the first of two and covers the Boeing Vertol Chinook, Aérospatiale Puma, Westland Sea King, Westland Wessex and Westland Whirlwind helicopters in Royal Air Force (RAF) service; British Army and Royal Navy (RN) helicopters will be in the next book in the series.

The Chinook, Puma and Wessex were used in the 1970s and '80s in the Support Helicopter (SH) role, mainly for the British Army. The Wessex replaced the Whirlwind in the Search and Rescue (SAR) role, as well as the Royal and VIP roles with The Queen's Flight. The Wessex was then replaced by the Sea King in the SAR role and Puma and Chinook in the SH role. On 31 March 1995, The Queen's Flight was disbanded, and its two Wessex transferred to 32 (The Royal) Sqn and were finally retired from royal duties on 1 April 1998. The author, on promotion to squadron leader in 1996, had HQ responsibility for the RAF's communication aircraft, namely those operated by 32 (The Royal) Sqn, so he got to know the two Wessex helicopters well!

These five helicopters were the true tactical transport workhorses of these two decades, well known in their bright yellow SAR paintwork and for the impact that the Chinook made in the Falklands War in 1982 (where SAR was also carried out by the Sea King – albeit in normal camouflage, not bright yellow). Meanwhile, the Puma and Wessex were active in the SH role across the globe in support of the British military.

First of all, I would like to thank Air Marshal Sir Baz North, KCB, OBE, who flew operationally the Wessex with 72 Sqn, the Chinook with 7 Sqn, the Chinook and Sea King with 78 Sqn (which he commanded) and Puma with 33 Sqn (which he also commanded), for agreeing to write the foreword. An ideal choice because of his considerable and impressive helicopter pedigree! I would like to yet again thank Bernd Rauchbach for checking the captions for me, and Andy Thomas for his continued advice and help on all things RAF. Yet again, this book is dedicated to the late David Howley, without whose generosity I would not have had access to so many photographs of aircraft he encountered, photographed and logged during his RAF career and afterwards.

Chris Goss
Marlow 2022

Chapter 1

Whirlwind

Above: Whirlwind HAR.10 XP338 first flew in November 1961 and was delivered to the RAF in January 1962. It is believed to have flown with 225 Sqn, the Central Flying School (CFS) and the Helicopter Development Unit (the latter being based at Old Sarum from 1961–1963). It was grounded at RAF Shawbury in 1980, was at RAF Cosford in 1984 and was still part of No. 2 School of Technical Training at RAF Cosford in 1990. It was scrapped in 1993. In this photo, it is coloured Day-Glo orange and silver.

Opposite: Whirlwind HAR.10 XP399 first flew in July 1962, after which it joined 230 Sqn at RAF Odiham. It was then damaged in an accident in Cyprus on 3 October 1964, after which it was repaired and allocated to 1563 Flt at RAF Akrotiri. Its subsequent history after that is unclear – the first photograph was taken at RAF Biggin Hill in September 1971, when it was flying with 32 Sqn at RAF Northolt, painted in the grey/blue/white standard Transport Command scheme. Shortly after, it went into storage, first at Wroughton in Wiltshire and then Pyrton Hill, Oxfordshire, and it was sold in 1976. It then became an attraction at a number of locations before ending up at The Wheatsheaf pub at Rettendon, Essex. It was first noted there in 1994 but had gone, presumably having been scrapped, by 2004.

Whirlwind HAR.2 XJ429 first flew in January 1955 and was delivered to the RAF the following month, first flying with the Aeroplane and Armament Experimental Establishment (A&AEE) for performance and handlings trials. By 1967, it had been converted to be a HAR.10 and was serving with 22 Sqn. It ended its days on the RAF Benson fire dump, having been destroyed by September 1979.

A Whirlwind HAR.4, believed to be XD165, overhead Usworth airfield, Durham. This aircraft was delivered in August 1954 and would later be converted to a HAR.10. In 1971, it was with 202 Sqn, but, by 1990, it was recorded as being a ground instructional airframe at RAF Halton. In 2000, it went to the Yorkshire Helicopter Preservation Group, but it was last reported in a very poor state at Caernarfon Airfield's fire dump in September 2021.

Seen at RAF Valley is this distinctive Whirlwind HAR.10 XP331 of No. 2 Flying Training School (FTS). It first flew in October 1961 and was delivered to the RAF the following month. It was eventually scrapped in 1985 and ended its days on the Otterburn Ranges in Northumberland.

Close up of the No. 2 FTS badge, seen on Whirlwind HAR.10 XP331.

The crew of Whirlwind HAR.10 XP405 practices winching. This aircraft was delivered in November 1962 and served with 228 Sqn, the CFS and No. 2 FTS. The badge on the door indicates this aircraft as belonging to the CFS, and this is reinforced by 'Central Flying School' appearing beneath it. It was broken up at Shorncliffe in Kent in 1993.

Photographed at RAF Abingdon in September 1980 is Whirlwind HAR.10 XP359. By this time, it was being used for ground instruction. It had entered RAF service in April 1962, but by 1990 it was dumped at RAF Stafford and would be scrapped at Dundonald two years later.

Awaiting its fate at RAF Akrotiri in September 1982 is this Whirlwind HAR.10 of 84 Sqn. This Squadron converted to the Wessex in 1982, so no doubt this aircraft is awaiting disposal. Note the variations of the 84 Sqn scorpion badge.

While the date and location of this accident is unknown, the 225 Sqn badge on the nose does indicate that this is pre-November 1965. Whirlwind HAR.10 XP361 has suffered a nose wheel collapse. This aircraft was delivered in May 1962 and flew with 225, 110, 103 and finally 22 sqns. By 1982, it was being used for ground instruction and was reported as being on the RAF Chivenor fire dump in 1982, but the following year it was at RAF Boulmer in Northumberland. In 1984, it moved to RAF Valley to be the gate guardian. However, by 1992, it was at RAF Coltishall but in 1996 was sold for spares and its remains scrapped the following year.

Whirlwind HAR.10 XP398 was delivered to the RAF in August 1962. It flew with 225 (seen here), 110, 103 and 202 sqns as well as 1563 Flt, after which it joined 84 Sqn in Cyprus in 1972. It was used for ground instruction until 1981, after which it was located at the St John's School at Episkopi in Cyprus by 1984. It then went into storage at RAF Shawbury, but by 1990 it had been bought by the Gatwick Aviation Museum. It appears that it is no longer there.

Seen at RAF El Adem in Libya is Whirlwind HAR.10 XP353. Little is known about this aircraft, apart from it was built in 1962, was with 202 Sqn in 1971 and was destroyed at the Fire School at RAF Catterick in 1984. However, keeping in mind that the RAF left El Adem in 1970, this aircraft, as seen here, is probably with 1564 Flt, which was formed at El Adem in May 1969 from D Flt 202 Sqn but was then disbanded in Cyprus in March 1970.

Above: Delivered to the RAF in January 1962, Whirlwind HAR.10 XP332 was lost in an accident on 13 May 1969. While serving with 28 Sqn, it suffered an engine failure and ditched into the Pearl River off Lan-Tau Island, Hong Kong. The three crew were rescued, and the aircraft recovered and subsequently written off.

Left and below: Seen at 84 Sqn's dispersal at RAF Akrotiri in August 1974, are two Whirlwind HAR.10s in totally different colours. The first sports camouflage and markings as it was being used for United Nations support, while the second sports the standard SAR yellow scheme.

Photographed at RAF Coningsby in June 1972 is Whirlwind HAR.10 XP344. Another aircraft built in 1962, it ended its days as a ground instructional airframe in 2002 at RAF North Luffenham. In 2018, there was talk of it being restored, but by then what was left of the airframe was in a very poor state. In the background below, Puma HC.1 XW231 can be seen.

Seen getting airborne from RAF Akrotiri in November 1978 is Whirlwind HAR.10 XP345 of 84 Sqn. Delivered in February 1962, it flew with the CFS, 202 Sqn, 1563 Flt and finally 84 Sqn. It was retired in 1982, and it was then used for ground instruction at Dhekelia in Cyprus before going into storage at RAF Shawbury in 1986. It was then sold to Melbourne Autos but in 1998 moved to the Yorkshire Helicopter Preservation Group, which restored it over the next 10 years. It can now be seen at the Aeroventure Museum in Doncaster.

Whirlwind HAR.10 XP403 of 202 Sqn is seen at RAF Finningley in July 1977. Delivered in October 1962, it ended its days in 1981 being used for battle damage repair at RAF Brüggen and was sold as scrap at Sennelager in Germany in 1991.

A close-up of 202 Sqn's mallard badge, RAF Finningley, July 1977.

Right and below: Whirlwind XD163 was a unique helicopter. Built in 1954 as an eight-seat Mk.4, it was the first Whirlwind to be delivered to the RAF. It then served with 155, 275 and 228 sqns, and between 1961 and 1964, it was converted to be a HAR.10. After a short period on SAR duties in the Mediterranean and Middle East, in 1966 it was allocated to No. 2 FTS, whose colours are seen here. Retired in 1979, it went into storage at Wroughton but in 1991 was sold to the Helicopter Museum at Weston-super-Mare. After extensive restoration, it can still be seen at the museum today.

Whirlwind XK969 was built as a HAR.2 and delivered in June 1956, and five months later found itself taking part in Operation *Musketeer* in November 1956, the Anglo-French plan to capture the Suez Canal, as part of the Joint Experimental Helicopter Unit, which became the Joint Helicopter Unit on 30 October 1956. It helped lift elements of 45 Commando from HMS *Ocean* to Port Said. Converted to be a HAR.10, it is seen here with 202 Sqn at RAF Coltishall in June 1978. It ended its days at RAF Odiham but in 1986 moved to RAF Manston and by 1991 had perished.

Another Whirlwind HAR.10 to suffer a similar fate as XK969 was XP333, seen here with No. 2 FTS at RAF Valley. Built as a HAR.10 and delivered in February 1962, it too ended its days at RAF Odiham in 1980/81, still in No. 2 FTS colours. It too went to RAF Manston but had perished by 1990.

Whirlwind HAR.10 XJ435 was built as a HAR.2 but converted to a HAR.10. These photographs were taken at RAF Akrotiri in September 1969. In 1971, it became the first Whirlwind HAR.10 to serve with 32 Sqn, part of RAF Air Support Command. It then became an instructional airframe at RAF Halton and was scrapped at Dishforth in 1998.

Photographed in 1970 is Whirlwind HAR.10 XP395. Delivered in 1962, it flew with 110, 230 and 225 sqns. It then flew with 22 Sqn and the SAR Training Unit (SARTU) and by 1984 had been withdrawn from service to be used for ground instruction at RAF Halton. It was sold for scrap in 1987, after which it was sunk in New England Quarry, Plympton. It is now believed to be dumped at what was RAF North Luffenham in Rutland.

Seen at Biggin Hill is Whirlwind HAR.10 XP353 of 202 Sqn, the badge of which can be seen on the door. It would be destroyed at the Fire School at RAF Catterick in 1984.

Whirlwind HAR.10 XJ429 first flew in January 1955 as a HAR.2, but it was converted to be a HAR.10 in 1967 and served with 22 Sqn. It ended its days on the RAF Benson fire dump, having been burnt by September 1979. This photograph was taken in 1974.

A Whirlwind HAR.10 overhead RAF Fairford, August 1974.

Photographed in September 1990 is Whirlwind HAR.10 XJ763. Built as a HAR.2 in 1956, it was converted to be a HAR.10. It is seen here in 32 Sqn colours. It was sold and given the registration G-BKHA in 1994, after which it went to the Wings of Eagles Discovery Centre, Elmira, New York. It sat outside for at least ten years, but it appears that it has now been repainted in US Coast Guard colours, although it still retains its RAF serial number.

An ignominious fate awaited Whirlwind HAR.10 XP360, seen here at RAF Valley in 1973. Delivered in 1962, it served with 225 Sqn and finally with the CFS, whose markings and colour scheme are seen here. Sold in 1976 to Showline Helicopters, it was stored in Kent before being displayed by the Second World War Aircraft Preservation Society at Lasham in Hampshire from 1980. In 2005, it was sold to the War Game Paintball Park, and it is now at the Oaker Wood Leisure paintballing centre near Leominster in Herefordshire.

Whirlwind Variants

HAR.2	33 built for RAF
HAR.4	24 built. Improved HAR.2 for use in hot-and-high terrain
HAR.10	68 built. Air transport and SAR

RAF Whirlwind Squadrons

22 Sqn	1955–81
28 Sqn	1968–72
32 Sqn	1970–81
84 Sqn	1972–82
103 Sqn	1963–72
110 Sqn	1963–71
155 Sqn	1954–59
202 Sqn	1964–79
225 Sqn	1961–65
228 Sqn	1962–64
230 Sqn	1962–71
275 Sqn	1959–59
1563 Flt	To 1972
1564 Flt	1969–70
CFS	
SARTU	
No. 2 FTS	

Chapter 2

Wessex

Left and below: Wessex HC.2 XR501 first flew in July 1963, joining the RAF the following month. It was one of four aircraft that joined the Intensive Flying Trials Unit for operational trials, before joining 18 Sqn (whose badge can be seen on the tail) in January 1964. It was later converted to a HAR.2, after which it served with 22 Sqn. In 1997, it went into storage at RAF Shawbury but in 2000 was reported as being at the RN's Air Engineering School (AES) at Gosport. It was then seen at Keogh Barracks, Aldershot before being acquired by Everett Aero at Sproughton in Essex in 2014. It is currently believed to be in private hands in France.

Wessex HC.2 XV728 first flew in April 1968, after which it served with 18 Sqn (seen in this photograph), CFS and No. 2 FTS. It also flew with 72 Sqn, where it acquired the unofficial name 'Argonaut'. After amassing 12,031 flying hours, it was assigned to the Defence Aviation Repair Agency (DARA) at Fleetlands in Hampshire in 1997, but the following year it was sold to the Newark Air Museum, Nottinghamshire, where it still remains in 2022.

Wessex HC.2 XR518 was delivered to the RAF in February 1964. It is seen here serving with 18 Sqn. In 1977, it was converted to a HAR.2 and served with 22 Sqn. Its flying days over, it was used for ground instruction at AES Gosport and was believed to have been scrapped in 2016.

Wessex HC.2 XR497 was delivered in February 1963 and was recorded as flying with 78 Sqn at Khormaksar in 1968, 103 Sqn at Tengah in 1973 and is seen here in 18 Sqn markings. In 1977, it was converted to be a HAR.2 and then flew with 22 and 202 sqns before ending its RAF career with 72 Sqn. In June 2002, it went to the Fuerza Aerea Uruguaya (Uruguayan Air Force) and flew with Escuadrón Aéreo n.°5 (Helicópteros). It is now on display at the Museo Aeronautico in Montevideo.

Another view of HC.2 XR501 of 18 Sqn on static display. In the background is Victor SR.2 XL193, which in 1971 was one of three Victors of 543 Sqn that took part in Operation *Attune*. Operating out of Lima Airport in Peru, they were modified to monitor radiation as a result of French atmospheric nuclear tests.

Wessex HC.2 XT601 first flew in March 1966 and was delivered to the RAF three months later. It served with the Khormaksar SAR Flt in 1966 and the Muharraq SAR Flt in 1967. It was also recorded as being with 72 Sqn in 1977 and then 22 Sqn in 1983. It ended its days as a ground instructional aircraft at RAF Odiham in 1997, after which it must have been scrapped.

Wessex HC.2 XT602 first flew in June 1966, and it too served with the Khormaksar and Muharraq SAR Flts. In 1974, it was one of two HC.2s of 72 Sqn modified for a purely SAR role (albeit when collected from DARA, it was forced to adopt a hybrid yellow/standard camouflage scheme). It then had a long service with 22 Sqn before being scrapped at Gosport in 2002.

Seen here at RAF Brize Norton is Wessex HC.2 XR502 in 60 Sqn markings. Built in 1963, it was one of four aircraft to join the Intensive Flying Trials Unit for operational trials in August 1963. The following month, it was seen at Biggin Hill airshow. Following disposal, in 2004 it was registered as G-CCUP, and then in 2013 it was registered as N486KA by International Air Services, Carson City. It is currently in private hands at Stonegate in East Sussex.

Wessex HC.2 XR505 first flew in 1963, joining the Short-Range Conversion Unit at RAF Odiham the following year. By 1983, it was with No. 2 FTS and went into storage at RAF Shawbury in 1997. The following year it was delivered to Aviacion Naval Uruguaya (Uruguayan Naval Aviation), where it flew as A-081 but still with the No. 2 FTS markings. In 2014, the Wessex Restoration Project began negotiations to acquire this Wessex, which last flew in 2010, but this had stalled by 2018 and the project appears to no longer exist.

Wessex HC.2 XV730 of 22 Sqn is seen at Middle Wallop airfield in 1989. It first flew in May 1968 and last flew with 84 Sqn at RAF Akrotiri in 2003, after which it went into storage at RAF Shawbury. In 2004, it was sold to the Classic Flyers Museum, Tauranga, New Zealand, where it can still be seen outside, in 84 Sqn colours.

Wessex HC.2 XT604 of 22 Sqn, RAF Fairford 1989. Delivered in 1966, it flew with the Khormaksar and Muharraq SAR Flts, 103 Sqn and 22 Sqn. By 1993, it was flying with the SARTU and last flew in 1995. It was sold in 2000, and two years later went to Air and Ground Aviation (Staffordshire), but the following year went to the East Midland Aeropark, Castle Donnington, Leicestershire, where it is still in 2022.

The badge of the SARTU, which was based at RAF Valley. The Wessex replaced the Whirlwind in 1985, and in 1997, the SARTU was amalgamated with the Defence Helicopter Flying School and exchanged its Wessex for the Bell Griffin HT.1.

Wessex HU.5 XT463 had quite a busy and varied career. Delivered to the RN in September 1965, it served with 845, 848 and 707 sqns. In 1982, it was then selected for 848 Sqn and would have gone to the Falkland Islands on the *Atlantic Conveyor* but was slightly damaged arriving in Plymouth and was replaced by another airframe. Following repairs, it went to the Falkland Islands on MV *Astronomer* arriving in July 1982. It was then converted to be a HU.5C, after which it joined 84 Sqn in Cyprus, where this photograph was taken. It returned in 1996 to Air Engineering and Survival School (AESS) Gosport, after which it went to Predannack in Cornwall. It was used for spares recovery by Air and Ground Aviation, Hixon, from 2000 onwards but had been scrapped by 2010.

Another Wessex HU.5 with a similar career was XS498. Delivered to the RN in 1964, it served with 845, 847, 707 and 772 sqns. It was in storage at Wroughton by 1982 but was brought out of storage to go to the Falkland Islands, returning to join 707 Sqn in July 1982. It too then joined 84 Sqn before going to AESS, then Predannack and finally Air and Ground Aviation, after which it was scrapped.

Seen at RAF Odiham in December 1971 is Wessex HC.2 XS674 of 72 Sqn. Delivered to the RAF in March 1965, it was reported with 78 Sqn in 1967 and 60 Sqn in 1996 as well as 18 Sqn. It is currently owned by Wessex Aviation and resides at Biggin Hill, still in 60 Sqn markings.

Wessex HAS.1 XM330 was delivered to the Ministry of Defence in December 1959 and spent the rest of its career on trials work with the A&AEE and from 1978 the Royal Aircraft Establishment (RAE) at Farnborough. In 1994, it went to the Helicopter Museum at Weston-super-Mare, where it can still be seen today.

Another RAE Wessex was this HAS.1 (later converted to HU.5), XL728. It first flew in September 1958, after which it appears to have remained with Westlands for engine development work before going into storage in 1966. By 1971, it was at RAE until 1985 when it went to the Pendine Ranges in Wales in 1986. It then appeared on the RAF Brawdy fire dump and had been scrapped by 1992.

Wessex HC.2 XR518 was delivered to the RAF in February 1964 and is seen here at RAF Mildenhall in August 1989 flying with 22 Sqn. It was a ground exhibit at the RAF Finningley Royal Review in July 1977 (still with 22 Sqn) but prior to this had been with 18 Sqn at RAF Gütersloh. It ended up being used for ground instruction at AESS Gosport and was presumed scrapped around 2016.

Another colourful RAE aircraft was Wessex HC.2 XR503, seen here in July 1989. Delivered in September 1963, it remained with the RAE on trials work until 2010, when it was at the RAF Manston Fire School for ground instruction. It was finally scrapped in 2020.

Above: Wessex HC.2 XV721 of 72 Sqn photographed during Exercise *Hardfall*, 1980. Delivered to the RAF in January 1968, it served with 72 and 18 sqns. It went into storage at RAF Shawbury in 2001 and in 2003 was exported to Uruguay where it was given the serial A-080.

Left: Another Wessex HC.2 of 72 Sqn in more normal camouflage. The serial of this aircraft is not visible.

Below: Photographed at RAF Odiham are Wessex HC.2s XR508 and XR519 of 72 Sqn. The former was delivered to the RAF in December 1963 and was last reported at AESS Gosport being used for ground instruction; it was scrapped in 2006. XR519 was delivered three months later. On 7 December 1990, and now with No. 2 FTS, the unit test pilot was carrying out a rotor turning ground run following maintenance. The aircraft then developed ground resonance (where lateral oscillation is triggered by forced or induced vibration associated with a helicopter in contact with the ground) and rolled over onto its port side. The two crewmen suffered slight injuries, and the Wessex was written off and later scrapped.

Coming into land at Keevil in June 1981 is Wessex HAR.2 XR501 of 22 Sqn. In 1997, it went into storage at RAF Shawbury but in 2000 was at AES at Gosport. It was then seen at Keogh Barracks Aldershot before being acquired by Everett Aero at Sproughton in Essex in 2014, and it is currently believed to be in private hands in France.

Photographed at RAF Odiham in May 1977 is Wessex HC.2 XV726 of 72 Sqn. Delivered in April 1968, its claim to fame was that it was initially used by The Queen's Flight for crew training. In 2016, it was reported as being acquired by The Wessex Club at Biggin Hill, where it still resides.

Wessex HC.2 XT674 of 72 Sqn is photographed in October 1968. This aircraft was delivered in February 1967 and served with 72 and 22 sqns. On 1 February 1987, it was assisting in airlifting an injured female from Ben Cruachan in Scotland but was diverted to Ben More and crashed when a rotor blade hit a rock. One of the crew was fatally injured, and three more were injured; sadly, the patient also died.

Wessex HC.2 XR516 of 18 Sqn seen at RAF Odiham. Delivered in February 1964, it served with 18 Sqn, No. 2 FTS and finally 60 Sqn. It went into storage at RAF Shawbury in 1999 but soon after went to AES at HMS Sultan. Ten years later, it was back at RAF Shawbury, where it is now the gate guardian.

Wessex HC.2 XV719 was delivered in December 1967. It flew with 72 Sqn and is seen here with 84 Sqn, whose aircraft carried badges of playing card suits on the tail. On 27 April 1990, this aircraft was back with 72 Sqn and hit the ground during a wing-over manoeuvre at Bishop's Court, Northern Ireland. The tail broke off, and the aircraft was subsequently written off. All three crew were injured.

Wessex HC.2 XV722, seen here with No. 2 FTS at RAF Alconbury in September 1983, was delivered to the RAF in February 1968, after which it flew with 18 and 72 sqns. It went into storage at RAF Shawbury in 1997 but, in 1999, was sold to Air and Ground Aviation where it was to be used for spares. It is now in private hands at Badger's Mount, Kent.

Wessex HC.2 XT680 of 22 Sqn getting airborne; the location and date are not known. This aircraft was delivered to the RAF in May 1967 and was finally grounded in January 2003. In 1973, it was flying with 103 Sqn and finally flew with 84 Sqn at RAF Akrotiri. It went into storage at RAF Shawbury but was sold to the Classic Flyers Museum in 2004.

Seen at Farnborough in August 1980 is Wessex HCC.4 XV732 of The Queen's Flight. It first flew in March 1969 and in June of the same year entered service with The Queen's Flight. It then had a long and distinguished career, and when The Queen's Flight was disbanded on 31 March 1995, was transferred to 32 (The Royal) Sqn at RAF Northolt. On 1 April 1998, both XV732 and sister aircraft XV733 were retired and went into storage at RAF Shawbury, but, in March 2002, XV732 was transported to the RAF Museum at Hendon. XV733 was sold in 2001 to the Helicopter Museum in Weston-super-Mare.

Wessex HC.2 XS677 of 230 Operational Conversion Unit (OCU) seen at RAF Abingdon in August 1980. Delivered to the RAF in April 1965, in 2001 it was sold to Wessex Air Ltd and given the serial ZK-HBE. In 2002, it was with Helilogging Ltd in New Zealand and in 2006 was with the Wessex Trust. It is now believed to be with the Classic Flyers Museum; in late 2020, was the subject of a legal case that had first begun in 2004.

Wessex HC.2 XS679 of 18 Sqn, RAF Wildenrath, 1978. Delivered in May 1965, it flew with 18 Sqn and No. 2 FTS before being sold to Uruguay in 1998 where it became A-084 with the Armada Nacional del Uruguay.

Wessex HC.2 XT675 of 72 Sqn seen at RAF Bassingbourn in May 1978. Delivered in March 1965, it was withdrawn from RAF service and went to Uruguay in June 1997 and was given the serial A-073.

Another 72 Sqn Wessex HC.2 seen at Bassingbourn in May 1978 was XR523. Delivered in July 1964, most of its life it flew with 72 Sqn. It is believed to have finally flown with 60 Sqn before being used for ground instruction at DARA in 1997 and then HMS Raleigh at Torpoint. It was last reported as being at the Pembrey Ranges, Carmarthenshire, in 2021.

Wessex Variants

HAS.1	140 built. Originally RN; later converted to HAS.3
HC.2	73 built. RAF troop carrier based on HAS.1
HAR.2	SAR conversion of HC.2
HCC.4	Two built. Royal/VIP
HU.5	101 built. RN troop carrier

RAF Wessex Squadrons

18 Sqn	1964–80
22 Sqn	1962–76
32 Sqn	1995–98
60 Sqn	1992–97
72 Sqn	1964–2002
78 Sqn	1965–71
84 Sqn	1982–2003
103 Sqn	1972–75
202 Sqn	1982–82
SARTU	
No. 2 FTS	
Khormaksar SAR Flt	
Muharraq SAR Flt	
The Queen's Flight	1969–95

Chapter 3

Sea King

Seen at RAF Waddington in 2002 is Sea King HAR.3 ZX596. The Sea King came into service with the RAF in 1978 as a replacement for the Whirlwind on SAR duties; this aircraft was built and delivered the same year and was part of the initial 19 procured. This aircraft flew initially with 202 Sqn, and in 1999 it was the first Sea King with 78 Sqn in the Falkland Islands to revert to the SAR yellow paint scheme. When RAF SAR was privatised in 2016, this aircraft was disposed of and is currently in storage with Heliops at Somerton in Somerset.

Seen at RAF Fairford in 2002 is Sea King HAR.3 XZ597. Delivered on August 1978, it flew with 22, 78, 202 and 203 sqns before being put up for sale in 2016. It was bought by Historic Helicopters Ltd, which have maintained it and registered it G-SKNG. Its first flight after restoration was in March 2020.

The 203 Sqn seahorse badge is seen on Sea King HAR.3 ZX597. 203 Sqn was reformed at RAF St Mawgan in 1996 as the Sea King OCU and was disbanded in 2014.

Another Sea King HAR.3 delivered in 1978 was XZ598. It suffered an accident at RAF Lossiemouth on 3 July 2006 when, following a tail rotor malfunction, it landed heavily, and the tail section was torn off. It was put up for disposal in 2016, after which it was bought to become the Sea King Cafe in Scarborough. In 2019, it was bought by a private collector and is now believed to be being restored at Myjava, Slovakia.

Photographed at Middle Wallop airfield in 1989 is Sea King HAR.3 XZ590. On the nose is the mallard badge of 202 Sqn. This aircraft first flew in January 1978 and was delivered to the RAF two months later. Today, it is another aircraft in storage with Heliops.

The Maltese cross and 'pi' symbol badge of 22 Sqn is seen on the nose of a Sea King HAR.3. 22 Sqn operated from RAF Chivenor in Devon, RAF Wattisham in Suffolk, RAF Valley in Anglesey and RAF Lossiemouth in Scotland. C Flt at RAF Valley shared its Sea Kings with the Sea King OCU. The squadron was disbanded in October 2015.

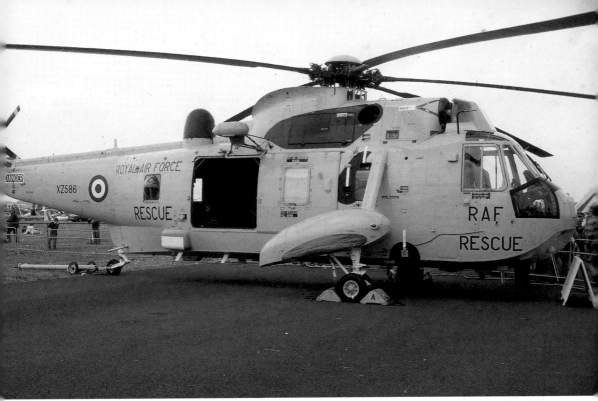

Sea King HAR.3 XZ586 of the RAF Sea King Training Unit (RAFSKTU) is seen at Farnborough in September 1978. First flown exactly a year before, it was the first HAR.3 to be delivered to the RAF in February 1978. It then served in the Falkland Islands, 22 and 202 sqns and 1564 Flt. It went into storage at Gosport in 2015 but is now stored by Heliops.

Photographed at Royal Naval Air Station (RNAS) Culdrose in March 1979 is Sea King HAR.3 XZ597 of 202 Sqn. Delivered in August 1978, it flew with 22, 78, 202 and 203 sqns, after which it was bought by Historic Helicopters in 2016.

Sea King HAR.3 XZ588 of the RAFSKTU, seen at RNAS Yeovilton in August 1979. Delivered in January 1978, in April 2015 it flew to DARA to be stored and was then used for ground instruction. In August 2020, it was sold to Lift West (Helicopters) Ltd, which then became Historic Helicopters Ltd, and given the registration G-SEAK.

Below, opposite and overleaf: Sea King HAR.3 XZ585 of 202 Sqn displaying at RAF Waddington in June 1980. It first flew in September 1977 and was delivered to the RAF January the following year. It served also with the RAFSKTU and 22 Sqn. On 28 January 1989, while serving with 202 Sqn, it lost an engine at low-level due to gearbox failure and suffered severe damage to the forward fuselage when it crash-landed at Craig Meagaidh, Loch Loggan, near Fort William. It was repaired at Fleetlands, after which it flew with 22 Sqn and then 202 Sqn. In April 2015, it flew from RAF Valley to Gosport to await disposal and, in December 2017 it was moved to the RAF Museum where it is still on display in 2022.

The 202 Sqn badge is seen on Sea King HAR.3 XZ595 at RAF Coltishall in June 1980. XZ595 was sold by Witham Specialist Vehicles in 2017 for £36,200 and now resides in a private collection at Charlwood in Surrey.

Right: Seen at Farnborough in September 1980 is Sea King HAR.3 XZ587. It joined the RAF in December 1977, and by the time this photograph was taken it was with 202 Sqn. It was grounded in August 2015, but the following January it went to the Cornwall Aviation Heritage Centre, Newquay, Cornwall Airport, also known as RAF St Mawgan.

Below: Seen overhead RAF Coltishall in September 1980 is Sea King HAR.3 XZ594 of 202 Sqn. On 27 April 1991, during a rescue attempt at Upper Eskdale in the Lake District, the rotors hit a cliff face and the helicopter crash-landed, its tail being broken off. All on board survived with minor injuries, and XZ594 was recovered and repaired. It is now stored by Heliops.

Seen at RAF Coltishall in September 1980 is Sea King HAR.3 ZA105 of 202 Sqn. Delivered earlier that same month, it served with the usual RAF Sea King units, and on 25 August 1982, departed Southampton on the MV *Contender Bezant* bound for the Falkland Islands. It was back in the Northern Hemisphere the following year. It is now stored by Heliops at Somerton in Somerset.

Seen this time at Keevil in September 1981 is Sea King HAR.3 ZA105, still with 202 Sqn.

Different colours. Seen on a sortie to Pebble Island in the Falklands on 20 July 1983 is Sea King HAR.3 XZ597, flying with C Flt 202 Sqn (which was based at RAF Coltishall). This aircraft now has the registration G-SKNG, and it is back to flying condition and owned by Historic Helicopters Ltd.

Sea King HAR.3 XZ586, seen with C Flt 202 Sqn in the Falkland Islands in summer 1983. The first HAR.3 to be delivered to the RAF in February 1978, it went into storage in Gosport in 2015 but is now in storage with Heliops at Somerton in Somerset.

Above, below and overleaf: A Sea King HAR.3, XZ588, coded SB, of C Flt 202 Sqn is coming in to land in the Falkland Islands in 1983. It is now owned by Historic Helicopters Ltd and has the registration G-SEAK.

Above, below and overleaf above: Sea King HAR.3 XZ599 of C Flt 202 Sqn, Navy Point, Port Stanley, in August 1983. Delivered in February 1979, it appears to have been an unlucky aircraft, having been slightly damaged in an accident while with 203 (R) Sqn at RAF St Mawgan on 16 August 2001, apparently while being flown by the station commander. It ended up on its side and was then repaired at Fleetlands, returning to 203 Sqn in late 2003. Then, on 22 October 2006, by this time with 22 Sqn, it suffered engine problems and force landed at Marske, North Yorkshire. This time it was repaired on site and took off again on 28 October 2006. It would be eventually stored at HMS Sultan in 2015 and is now believed to have been scrapped.

Below: Sea King HAR.3 XZ588 of C Flt 202 Sqn takes off over XZ597, Falkland Islands, 1983. The Sea King Detachment would become 1564 (Tactical Support) Flt in August 1983 and in May 1986 merged with 1310 Flt, which was flying Chinooks to become 78 Sqn. It would later be commanded by Sqn Ldr Baz North, who kindly wrote the foreword to this book, from July 1991 to September 1992.

Photographed at Middle Wallop airfield in July 1982 is Sea King HC.4X XV370 of the Empire Test Pilot's School (ETPS). Delivered to the UK in 1966, it spent much of its life on trials work with Westlands, the RAE, the A&AEE and the ETPS. In August 1989, it was withdrawn from use, only to be transferred to the RN the following year as a ground instructional airframe. It is currently still at the Defence School of Maritime Engineering at HMS Sultan.

Another 'raspberry ripple' Sea King was Mk.4X ZB506, seen here being operated by RAE Bedford and at Fairford in July 1989. Again, it was used for trials from December 1982 with the RAE, Defence Evaluation and Research Agency (DERA) and Defence Research Agency. It was last recorded as a film prop at White Waltham Airfield in Berkshire in 2022.

Built in 1986, Sea King Mk.4 ZF115, seen here with the ETPS at Boscombe Down in June 1990, had a varied career with the A&AEE and DERA. On 30 November 2001, it was damaged in an accident at Boscombe Down, but after repair, it joined the RN in 2009, serving with 849 Sqn, after which it was used for ground instruction at HMS Sultan, where it is still in 2022.

Sea King HAR.3 XZ590 of 202 Sqn is seen at Fairford in July 1989. In the background is the aircraft it was to replace, the Wessex. XZ590 is in storage with Heliops.

Sea King HAR.3 ZA105 of 202 Sqn. Delivered in September 1980, it served with the usual RAF Sea King units in the UK and Falkland Islands. It is now stored by Heliops at Somerton in Somerset.

Seen over the Falkland Islands in 1983 is this Sea King HAR.3 of C Flt 202 Sqn, soon to be 1564 Flt. This is believed to be XZ597.

Sea King Variants

HAR.3	19 built. SAR version for RAF
HC.4X	One used by Empire Test Pilot's School
Mk.4X	Two used for trials
SH-3D	US designation

RAF Sea King Squadrons

22 Sqn	1997–2015
78 Sqn	1986–2007
202 Sqn	1978–2015
203 Sqn (formerly Sea King OCU)	1996–2014
1564 Flt	1983–86
RAF Sea King Training Unit	1977–96

Chapter 4
Puma

Photographed outside the air terminal at RAF Brize Norton is Puma HC.1 XW201/DL. First flown in February 1971, it is known to have served with 240 OCU in 1983 and 1992, 33 Sqn in 1991 and 230 Sqn in 2002. The tiger badge on the door indicates this photograph was taken when it was with 230 Sqn. In 2011, it was being used for ground instruction and battle damage repair at RAF Benson and was scrapped in 2021.

Seen at RAF Chivenor in August 1972 is Puma HC.1 XW207/CD of 33 Sqn. First flown in May 1971, it joined the RAF and 33 Sqn the following month, after which it served with 1563 Flt in Belize and 230 Sqn. On 19 April 2000, XW207 was taking part in an exercise, and as it descended to deploy troops the tail rotor struck the ground; it became airborne again, but flight was seriously affected. The main blades then struck the ground, and it crashed on Hipswell Moor, Richmond, North Yorkshire, and rolled over coming to rest on its starboard side. It was repaired and re-joined 33 Sqn, but in 2012 it was in storage at RAF Shawbury and two years later had been used for spares and scrapped.

Puma HC.1 XW208/CE was built in 1971 and then served with 33 and 230 sqns and 1563 Flt before going into storage at RAF Shawbury in 2012. It was reported then as being used for ground instruction at RAF Cranwell in 2014, but in 2018 it was sold to the Newark Air Museum, where it can still be seen in 2022.

Puma HC.1 XW199 was the second Puma to be delivered to the RAF in 1971 and served with 240 OCU, 230, 33, 27(R) and 72 sqns and 1563 Flt. It was converted to an HC.2 in 2016 and is still flying with 28 Sqn at RAF Benson in 2022.

Seen overhead Duxford in July 1975 is a very new and clean Puma HC.1. The serial and squadron are unknown.

Puma HC.1 XW225 of 230 Sqn. Built in 1972, it also served with 240 OCU and 33 Sqn. On 15 February 1997, it was serving with 18 Sqn at RAF Laarbruch and hit trees during landing at night in snow fall and crashed near Urspring in Bavaria, Germany. Sadly, the pilot was fatally injured. It was sold for scrap in 2003, but in 2019 the cabin arrived at the Newark Air Museum. The following year, it went to be a training aid at the Beckenham Training Camp in Lincolnshire.

Puma HC.1 XW228 of 230 Sqn seen at Greenham Common in August 1976. Built in 1972, it first flew with 230 Sqn, but three years later it was with 33 Sqn. On 27 December 1979, while on Operation *Agila* in Rhodesia (now Zimbabwe), during a flight from New Sarum to Kotwa, it struck telegraph wires near Mtoko, crashed and burnt out. Sadly, all three crew were killed.

Puma HC.1 XW205 of 33 Sqn, seen at RAF Odiham in May 1977 for the squadron's 60th anniversary. Eight months later, on 30 January 1978, while on exercise in Norway, the starboard cabin door came off, hit the tail rotor and the Puma crashed near Voss; all three crew unfortunately lost their lives.

Another Puma on display at 33 Sqn's 60th Anniversary was HC.1 XW206. Built in 1971, it also flew with 27 Sqn. It went into storage at RAF Shawbury in 2012 but was scrapped two years later.

Puma HC.1 XW208 can still be seen today. Built in 1971, it had a long career with 33 and 230 sqns and 1563 Flt on Operation *Telic*. In 2012, it in went into storage at RAF Shawbury and two years later became a ground instructional airframe at RAF Cranwell. In 2018, it went to Newark Air Museum, where it has been restored.

Seen in a distinctive scheme is Puma HC.1 XW211 of 33 Sqn, RAF Odiham, May 1977. Built in 1971, it suffered two accidents during its career. On 15 April 2007, while flying with 1563 Flt in Iraq, it suffered Category 4 damage when its main blades intertwined with XW218. Repaired by September 2009, on 5 July 2011 and now with 33 Sqn, it took off from Middle Wallop airfield headed for RAF Benson, but three minutes after take-off, the main gear box cover flew off and hit the main and rear rotor blades and an emergency landing was made adjacent to the Walworth Business Park at Andover. The Puma landed first on its port undercarriage, yawed, rolled onto its side and the tail broke off. It was scrapped three years later. The second photograph shows unofficial artwork on the nose.

Puma HC.1 XW235 of 230 Sqn seen at Greenham Common in June 1977. It had been built five years previously, was upgraded to an HC.2 in 2013 and is still flying from RAF Benson in 2022. The second photograph shows the 230 Sqn tiger badge.

Puma HC.1 XW231 of 33 Sqn, photographed at RAF Coningsby in June 1977, has had a long career. Built in 1972, it has also flown with 230 OCU and 230 Sqn. Upgraded to an HC.2 in 2013, it is now operated jointly by 28, 33 and 230 sqns at RAF Benson, 50 years after it was built.

Participating at the helicopter flypast at RAF Finningley for the Queen's Jubilee Review in July 1977 is Puma HC.1 XW226 of 230 Sqn. Another Puma built in 1972, it also flew with 27, 33 and 18 sqns and 1563 Flt. It went into storage at RAF Shawbury in 2014.

Seen at RNAS Yeovilton in 1977 is Puma HC.1 XW229 of 230 Sqn. Built in 1972, it would be upgraded to an HC.2. On 11 October 2015, it struck the tether of a Persistent Threat Detection System and crashed onto a road junction at the NATO HQ in Kabul. Sadly, five onboard lost their lives and another four were injured, together with a bystander on the ground.

Displaying at Middle Wallop airfield is Puma HC.1 XW216 of 33 Sqn. Built in 1971, it also flew with 230 and 18 sqns and 1563 Flt. It was converted to an HC.2 in 2012 and took part in the Puma 50th Anniversary flypast on 7 July 2021.

Seen at Farnborough in September 1982 is HC.1 ZA941 flown by the RAE. This aircraft was the only one not operated by the RAF. On 8 August 1991, ZA941 crashed one mile south of Camp de Canjeurs airbase in southeast France during a post-maintenance flight. Two on board were killed, and another two badly injured.

Puma HC.1 XW236 of 33 Sqn displaying at Farnborough in September 1982. Again serving with 33, 18 and 230 sqns, after a career lasting 42 years, in 2014 it became a ground instructional airframe at RAF Brize Norton and was reported as being on the fire dump in October 2021.

Troops fast-roping from a Puma HC.1 of 230 Sqn. Date and location are not known, neither is the Puma's serial number.

A very weather-beaten Puma HC.1 XW220 of 33 Sqn is seen at Fairford in July 1991. Built in 1971, it was converted to be an HC.2 in 2015. It is still on active service at RAF Benson but did not take part in the Puma 50th Anniversary flypast on 7 July 2021.

Seen at RAF Odiham in May 1987 is Puma HC.1 XW202, which had, until recently, been flying with 1563 Flt in Belize. It went into storage at RAF Shawbury in 2009, but in 2014 it went to Strenshall Barracks, North Yorkshire, where it still can be found today.

Below and opposite: Built in 1972, Puma HC.1 XW224 was repainted a number of times. Seen here at Fairford in July 1991, in a unique 230 Sqn scheme, it had previously flown with 72, 33 and 18 sqns and would take part in Operation *Telic*. By now an HC.2, it would again be painted in tiger livery in 2018 to celebrate 100 years of 230 Sqn, and in July 2021 it would be repainted in the colour scheme adopted when the Puma first entered service and have a union flag on the tail, badges of all squadrons that had flown the Puma painted on the engine housing and a bespoke 'Puma 50' badge on the door. It is still flying from RAF Benson in 2022.

Seen at RAF Odiham in May 1977 celebrating 33 Sqn's 60th anniversary is Puma HC.1 XW233. On 26 November 1992, this aircraft was with 230 Sqn and collided on landing at Bessbrook Mill, Northern Ireland, with Gazelle ZB681 of 665 Sqn. Unfortunately, there were four fatal casualties in the Puma and two seriously injured in the Gazelle.

Puma HC.1 XW219 first flew in November 1971 and was delivered the following month. Converted to an HC.2 in 2014, it is believed to be stored at RAF Benson. This aircraft has been immortalised as a Corgi model.

Puma HC.1 XW200 of 240 Sqn seen at RAF Brize Norton in June 1982. It had served with the Helicopter Operational Conversion Flt after delivery to the RAF in 1971, then 240 OCU, 27 and 230 sqns and finally 33 Sqn. On 9 April 2001, it crashed at Kacanik, Kosovo, three minutes after take-off. Its remains were then stored at RAF Shawbury.

Seen at RAF Upper Heyford in August 1983 is Puma HC.1 XW232 of 230 Sqn. Again, built in 1972, it had a full career with 33 and 230 sqns before being the first conversion to an HC.2 in 2012. It is still on active service at RAF Benson

Puma HC.1 XW237 of 33 Sqn getting airborne from Farnborough September 1986. This would be converted to an HC.2 in 2014 and took part in the Puma 50th Anniversary flypast on 7 July 2021.

Cockpit of a Puma HC.1. Date, location, serial and squadron are not known.

Photographed at RAF Odiham in September 1972 is a Puma HC.1 of 230 Sqn.

Seen at Greenham Common in 1974 is Puma HC.1 XW213. Built in 1972, it was converted to an HC.2 standard in 2014 and is still operational at RAF Benson.

Puma Variants

HC.1   Initial order based on SA 330E. 40 ordered with eight attrition replacements

HC.2   24 upgraded. Totally rebuilt HC.1 with more powerful engines, glass cockpit, new avionics, secure communications and improved self-defence suite

RAF Puma Squadrons

18 Sqn	1992–97 (partial equipment)
27 (R) Sqn	1993–98 (partial equipment)
28 Sqn	2009–current (partial equipment)
33 Sqn	1971–current
72 Sqn	1997–2002 (partial equipment)
230 Sqn	1971–current
1563 Flt	1981–93; 2004–09
240 OCU	1971–93 (becomes 27 (R) Sqn)

Chapter 5

Chinook

Above: Chinook HC.1 ZA711 was built in 1981 and delivered to the RAF in November of the same year. It then served with 18 Sqn (seen here in 2002, after it had been converted to an HC.2 in 1999) and 7 Sqn as well as 78 Sqn in the Falkland Islands in 1989. It was later converted to an HC.4 and is still being operated by the Chinook Wing at RAF Odiham as an HC.6A.

Right: A close-up of the 18 Sqn badge on Chinook HC.2 ZA711.

Chinook HC.1 ZA675 of 18 Sqn moving Rapier surface-to-air missile equipment; the date and location is not known. This aircraft was finally converted to an HC.6A and is still active at RAF Odiham.

Seen at RNAS Yeovilton in August 1981 is Chinook HC.1 ZA676 of 240 OCU. On 14 November 1984, it struck trees, rolled 140 degrees, and ended up at a bottom of a clearing at Cranborne Wood, Micheldever, Hampshire. Of the seven on board, just two were injured and the aircraft was struck off charge, becoming a ground instruction airframe at RAF Odiham. It was last reported at RAF Manston in 1996 and has since been destroyed.

Photographed in September 1981 is Chinook HC.1 ZA673 of 240 OCU. It would be converted to an HC.2, but on 30 August 2009, and now with 1310 Flt, it was damaged in a heavy landing six miles east of Sangin, Helmand Province, Afghanistan, and was destroyed by explosives to prevent its capture by the Taliban.

Below and overleaf: A series of photographs showing ZA679/BV and ZA680/BW demonstrating the capabilities of the Chinook. Taken in October 1981, this 18 Sqn Chinook is seen picking up an 8.7-tonne FV104 Samaritan, the armoured ambulance version of the Combat Vehicle Reconnaissance Tracked (CVRT).

Chinook HC.1 ZA709 of 18 Sqn seen at RNAS Yeovilton in July 1982. On 19 August 2009, this aircraft, now an HC.2, was with 1310 Flt in Afghanistan and had to make a forced landing in the Sangin area due to an engine fire, possibly caused by being hit by a rocket propelled grenade. The four crew and 15 passengers escaped and were rescued by another Chinook. ZA709 was then destroyed by an air strike.

Left and below: Chinook HC.1 ZA673 of 240 OCU displaying at RAF Odiham, September 1982. This aircraft was lost in Afghanistan on 30 August 2009.

Seen at Farnborough in September 1982 are Chinook HC.1 ZA710/BC and ZA711/BR, each with 7 Sqn's badge on the tail. Both were delivered in 1981, and both would be eventually converted to HC.6As in 2018. They are still operational in 2022.

Chinook HC.1 ZA721 of 18 Sqn at Farnborough September 1982. On 27 February 1987, this aircraft was with 78 Sqn and crashed on a test flight after servicing, six miles southeast of RAF Mount Pleasant Airport in the Falkland Islands. The cause has never been fully determined, and sadly all seven on board lost their lives.

Chinook HC.1 ZA714 of 7 Sqn, seen at RAF Upper Heyford in May 1990. This aircraft was delivered in January 1982 and has now been converted to an HC.6A and is still operational.

Chinook HC.1 ZA671 of 7 Sqn is seen at RAF Odiham in June 1989, with a newly painted aft pylon, celebrating 75 years of 7 Sqn. This was the display aircraft for 1989 and was normally flown by Flt Lt Mal Reeves that display season. Delivered in November 1980, on 7 April 2012, this aircraft, now an HC.2 and operated by C Flt 27 Sqn, crashed in the Yuma/El Centro desert, California. There were no major injuries among the crew or passengers, but the aircraft suffered extensive damage. However, ZA671 was repaired and is still flying in 2022, having been modified to an HC.6A.

Seen overhead the bleak landscape of the Falkland Islands in August 1983 is a Chinook HC.1 of what was informally known as CHINDET (CHINook DETatchment). Later this same month, CHINDET would be formally known as 1310 Flt.

Seen in August 1983 is the most well-known Chinook HC.1, ZA718, more commonly known as *Bravo November*. One of four Chinooks on board the MV *Atlantic Conveyor*, ZA718 was airborne on 25 May 1982 when the ship was hit by an Exocet missile and sank. ZA718 then landed on HMS *Hermes* and would be the only heavy lift helicopter available for the remainder of the Falklands War. It would later be involved in Iraq and Afghanistan. Upgraded throughout its life eventually to HC.6A, following its retirement, in March 2022, it was transported to the RAF Museum at Cosford for preservation and display.

Another Chinook HC.1, seen at Port Stanley in August 1983, was ZA707, seen here with the penguin badge adopted by 1310 Flt below the tail rotor. Delivered in 1981, it was offloaded at Ascension Island from the *Atlantic Conveyor* on 5 May 1982. after which it embarked on MV *Contender Bezant* to join with ZA718/BN. Upgraded throughout its life to now being an HC.6A, it is still operational from RAF Odiham in 2022.

Seen at Farnborough in September 1982 is Chinook HC.1 ZA708. On the port side, it has 18 Sqn's badge, on the starboard 7 Sqn's badge. On 10 August 2010, and by now modified to HC.2A and flying with 1310 Flt, it was involved in an accident at Bahdur in Helmand Province. Badly damaged, it was recovered to the UK at the end of the month for repair. It has now been modified to HC.6A and is still operational.

Chinook HC.1 ZA683 of 7 Sqn seen at RAF Brize Norton in June 1983. On 28 July 2020, this aircraft, now an HC.6A and flying with 18 Sqn, suffered a wire strike and force landed at Berthlwyd Farm, Llangynin, Carmarthenshire, having damage to the nose and all three cockpit windows. Damage repaired, ZA683 is still operational from RAF Odiham in 2022. ZA683 was the Chinook HC.2 chosen in 2016 to have its aft pylon coloured yellow and green and emblazoned with an elephant to commemorate the centenary of 27 Sqn.

Seen at RAF Odiham is Chinook HC.1 ZA674 of 240 OCU. The OCU's hummingbird badge is seen on the nose.

240 OCU's badge is seen on the tail of Chinook HC.1 ZD575. Delivered in October 1984, it was damaged by small arms fire near Musa Qalah on 17 May 2008. It is still operational in 2022 as an HC.6A.

Chinook HC.1 ZD980 of 240 OCU, Middle Wallop, July 1988. Delivered in 1985, it is now an HC.6A and still operational. On 23 November 1999, while on exercise at Soz in Oman, the aft pylon was ripped off when the 20-degree nose high attitude was exceeded.

Chinook HC.1 ZA704 of 240 Sqn displaying at Boscombe Down in June 1990. Delivered in 1981, it is still operational as an HC.6A.

Delivered in 1981, Chinook HC.1 ZA707 of 7 Sqn is seen here sporting unusual camouflage adopted by Special Forces Chinooks during the Gulf War from August 1990 to February 1991. These photographs were taken at Mildenhall in May 1991. Now an HC.6A, it is still flying operationally in 2022.

Chinook Variants 1970–89

HC.1	Initial purchase of 38. Based on CH-47C
HC.2	Based on CH-47D; HC.1 returned to Boeing for upgrade, initial aircraft back in service 1993. Three additional aircraft ordered for delivery in 1995. Six more ordered in 1995 to be HC.2A (later called HC.3)

RAF Chinook Squadrons

7 Sqn	1982–current
18 Sqn	1981–current
27 Sqn	1993–current
28 Sqn	2015–current
78 Sqn	1986–2007 (partial equipment)
1310 Flt	1982–current
240 OCU	1981–93

Other books you might like:

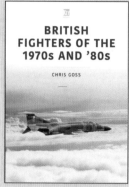

Historic Military Aircraft
Series, Vol. 2

Historic Military Aircraft
Series, Vol. 4

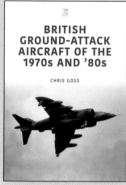

Historic Military Aircraft
Series, Vol. 8

Historic Military Aircraft
Series, Vol. 10

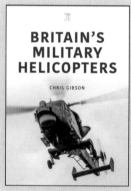

Modern Military Aircraft
Series, Vol. 4

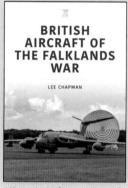

Historic Military Aircraft
Series, Vol. 13

For our full range of titles please visit:
shop.keypublishing.com/books

VIP Book Club
Sign up today and receive
TWO FREE E-BOOKS

Be the first to find out about our forthcoming
book releases and receive exclusive offers.

Register now at keypublishing.com/vip-book-club

*Our VIP Book Club is a 100% spam-free zone, and we will never share your email with anyone else.
You can read our full privacy policy at: privacy.keypublishing.com*